# CHIPS WITH EVERYTHING

# CHIPS
## WITH
# EVERYTHING

*A Play in two Acts*

*by*

ARNOLD WESKER

JONATHAN CAPE
THIRTY BEDFORD SQUARE
LONDON

FIRST PUBLISHED 1962
REPRINTED 1962
REPRINTED 1966
© 1962 BY ARNOLD WESKER

★

The song *The Cutty Wren*, which appears on page 39, is reprinted from *If I had a Song*, a collection of children's songs published by the Workers' Music Association, 136A Westbourne Terrace, London, w.2

PRINTED IN GREAT BRITAIN BY
LOWE AND BRYDONE (PRINTERS) LIMITED, LONDON
ON PAPER MADE BY JOHN DICKINSON AND CO. LTD
BOUND BY A. W. BAIN AND CO. LTD, LONDON

*Chips With Everything* was first presented by the English Stage Company Ltd at the Royal Court Theatre on April 27th, 1962, with the following cast:

| | |
|---|---|
| Corporal Hill | FRANK FINLAY |
| 239 Cannibal, Archie | GEORGE INNES |
| 252 Wingate (Chas) | COLIN CAMPBELL |
| 276 Thompson (Pip) | JOHN KELLAND |
| 247 Seaford (Wilfe) | LAURIE ASPREY |
| 284 McClure, Andrew | ALEXANDER BALFOUR |
| 272 Richardson (Whitey) | COLIN FARRELL |
| 277 Cohen (Dodger) | HUGH FUTCHER |
| 266 Smith (Dickey) | JOHN BULL |
| 279 Washington (Smiler) | RONALD LACEY |
| Wing Commander | MARTIN BODDEY |
| Squadron Leader | ROBERT BRUCE |
| Pilot Officer | CORIN REDGRAVE |
| P.T. Instructor Flt Sgt | MICHAEL GOLDIE |
| Recruit | PETER KELLY |
| Night Guard | BRUCE HEIGHLEY |
| 1st Corporal | ROGER HEATHCOTT |
| 2nd Corporal | MICHAEL BLACKHAM |
| 1st Airman | MICHAEL CRAZE |
| 2nd Airman | ALAN STEVENS |

Directed by John Dexter

*To*

*JOHN DEXTER*

*who has helped me to understand the theatre of my plays and directed them all when most others said they would fail.*

# CAST

*Conscripts*

    ARCHIE CANNIBAL 239
    WINGATE (CHAS) 252
    THOMPSON (PIP) 276
    SEAFORD (WILFE) 247
    ANDREW McCLORE 284
    RICHARDSON (GINGER) 272
    COHEN (DODGER) 277
    SMITH (DICKEY) 266
    WASHINGTON (SMILER) 279

*Officers*

    CORPORAL HILL
    WING COMMANDER
    SQUADRON LEADER
    PILOT OFFICER
    P.T. INSTRUCTOR, FLT SGT

    GUARD
    NIGHT CORPORAL
    1ST CORPORAL
    2ND CORPORAL
    AIRMAN

# ACT ONE

# ACT TWO

# ACT ONE

## Scene 1

*An R.A.F. hut. Nine new conscripts enter. They are subdued, uncertain, mumbling.* CORPORAL HILL *appears at door, stocky, Northern, collarless man. He waits till they notice him, which they gradually do till mumbling ceases, utterly – they rise to attention. After a long pause –*

HILL. That's better. In future, whenever an N.C.O. comes into the hut, no matter who he is, the first person to see him will call out 'N.C.O.!' 'N.C.O.!' like that. And whatever you're doing, even if you're stark rollock naked, you'll all spring to attention as fast as the wind from a duck's behind, and by Christ that's fast. Is that understood? (*No reply.*) Well is it? (*A few murmers.*) When I ask a question I expect an answer. (*Emphatically.*) Is that understood!

ALL (*shouting*). Yes, Corporal!

HILL. Anyone been in the Air Cadets? Any of the cadets? Anyone twenty-one or more then? Nineteen? (*Two boys,* ANDREW *and* DICKEY, *raise their hands. To one.*) Month you were born?

ANDREW. July, Corporal.

DICKEY. May, Corporal.

HILL (*to* DICKEY). You're senior man. (*To* ANDREW.) You're assistant. Shift your kit to top of hut. Not now – later.

(HILL *scrutinizes the rest. He lays his hand on the two smallest –* DODGER *and* GINGER.)

These small boys, these two, they're my boys. They'll do the jobs I ask them when I ask them; not much, my fires each day, perhaps my bunk – my boys. But they won't do my polishing – I do that myself. No one is to start on

11

them, no one is to bully them, if they do, then they answer to me. (*Pause.*) You can sit now.

(*Reads out list of names, each recruit rises and sits as called. Boys sit on their beds, waiting;* HILL *paces up and down, waiting his time. Then –* )

Right, you're in the R.A.F. now, you're not at home. This hut, this place here, this is going to be your home for the next eight scorching weeks. This billet here, you see it? This? It's in a state now, no one's been in it for the last four days so it's in a state now. (*Pause.*) But usually it's like a scorching palace! (*Pause.*) That's the way I want it to be cos that's the way it's always been. Now you've got to get to know me. My name is Corporal Hill. I'm not a very happy man, I don't know why. I never smile and I never joke – you'll soon see that. Perhaps it's my nature, perhaps it's the way I've been brought up – I don't know. The R.A.F. brought me up. You're going to go through hell while you're here, through scorching hell. Some of you will take it and some of you will break down. I'm warning you – some of you shall end up crying. And when that happens I don't want to see anyone laughing at him. Leave him alone, don't touch him.

But I'll play fair. You do me proud and I'll play fair. The last lot we 'ad 'ere 'ad a good time, a right time, a right good scorching time. We 'ad bags o' fun, bags o' it. But I will tear and mercilessly scratch the scorching daylights out of anyone who smarts the alec with me – and we've got some 'ere. I can see them, you can tell them. I count three already, you can tell them, by their faces, who know it all, the boys who think they're GOOD. (*Whispered.*) It'll be unmerciful and scorching murder for them – all. Now, you see this wireless here, this thing with knobs and a pretty light that goes on and off? Well that's ours, our wireless for this hut and for this hut only because this hut has always been the best hut. No other hut has a wireless. I want to keep that. I like music and I want to keep that wireless. Some people, when they get up in the morning, first thing all they want to do is smoke, or drink tea – not me, I've got to have music, the noise of instruments.

Everyone's got a fad, that's mine, music, and I want to be spoilt, you see to it that I'm spoilt. Right, if there's anyone here who wants to leave my hut and go into another because he doesn't like this 'un, then do it now, please. Go on, pick up your kit and move. I'll let 'im. (*No movement.*) You can go to the N.A.A.F.I. now. But be back by ten thirty, cos that's bleedin' lights out. (*Moves to door, pauses.*) Anyone object to swearing? (*No reply. Exits.*)

(*Stunned. A boy rushes in from another hut.*)

BOY. What's your'n say?

SMILER (*imitating*). My name is Corporal Hill, I'm not a happy man.

BOY (*imitating a Scotsman*). My name is Corporal Bridle – and I'm a bastard!

### Scene 2

*The N.A.A.F.I. One boy strumming a guitar.*

WILFE.   Dear mother come and fetch me
      Dear mother take me home
      I'm drunk and unhappy
      And my virginity's gone.

      My feet are sore and I'm weary
      The sergeant looks like dad
      O a two bob bit would buy me a nip
      And a N.A.A.F.I. girl in my bed.

13

Now Eskimo Nell has gone back to the land
Where they know how to – Eight weeks!
EIGHT STUPID WEEKS, MOTHER!

CHAS. I've left two girls at home, two of them, and I've declared passionate love to them both – both. Poor girls, promised I'd marry them when it was all over. They'll miss me.

WILFE. Wouldn't be so bad if my mother could hear me, but she's as deaf as a bat.

PIP. Bats are blind.

WILFE. Oh dear me, bats are blind, deary, deary me fellows.

PIP. Look old son, you're going to have me for eight painful weeks in the same hut, so spend the next five minutes taking the mickey out of my accent, get it off your chest and then put your working-class halo away because no one's going to care – O.K.?

CHAS. Where are you from then?

PIP. My father is a banker, we hate each other. I was born in a large country house and I'm scorching rich.

CHAS. You're going to do officer training then?

PIP. No! My father was also a general!

WILFE.    O my father was a general
          And I'm a general's son
          But I got wise to the old man's lies
          And kicked him up his you know, you
          know, you know, you know what I mean.
          Now Eskimo Nell has gone back to the land –
          EIGHT STUPID WEEKS, MOTHER!

SMILER. Give over, Wilfe, give over.

GINGER. Well roll on Christmas, roll on I say.

DODGER. So what then? You'll be back after four days, and then four more weeks of this –

GINGER. But I'll be married.

DODGER. You'll be what?

14

GINGER. I'm getting married two weeks from tomorrow –

CHAS. Bleedin' daft to get married. I got two girls back home, one's blonde and one's dark – it's the Jekyll and Hyde in me. Married? Bleedin' daft!

PIP. You mean you can actually think of better things to do than produce babies?

CHAS. You shut your classical mouth you, go away, 'oppit! 'Oppit or I'll lay you down. I haven't liked you from the start.

PIP. Oh sit down, there's a good boy, I wouldn't dream of fighting you.

SMILER. You don't mind being a snob, do you?

PIP. One day, when I was driving to my father's office, the car broke down. I could have got a taxi I suppose, but I didn't. I walked. The office was in the City, so I had to walk through the East End, strange – I don't know why I should have been surprised. I'd seen photographs of this Mecca before – I even used to glance at the *Daily Mirror* now and then, so God knows why I should have been surprised. Strange. I went into a café and drank a cup of tea from a thick, white, cracked cup and I ate a piece of tasteless currant cake. On the walls I remember they had photographs of boxers, autographed, and they were curling at the edges from the heat. Every so often a woman used to come to the table and wipe it with a rag that left dark streaks behind which dried up into weird patterns.Then a man came and sat next to me – WHY should I have been surprised? I'd seen his face before, a hundred times on the front pages of papers reporting a strike. A market man, a porter or a docker. No, he was too old to be a docker. His eyes kept watering, and each time they did that he'd take out a neatly folded handkerchief, unfold it and, with one corner, he'd wipe away the moisture, and then he'd neatly fold it up again and replace it in his pocket. Four times he did that, and each time he did it he looked at me and smiled. I could see grains of dirt in the lines of his face, and he wore an old waistcoat with pearl buttons. He wasn't untidy, the cloth even seemed a good cloth, and though his hair was thick with oil it was clean. I can even remember the colour of the walls, a pastel pink on the top half and turquoise blue on the bottom, peeling. Peeling in fifteen different places actually, I counted them. But what I couldn't understand was why I should have been so surprised. It wasn't as though I had been cradled in my childhood. And then I saw the menu, stained with tea and beautifully written by a foreign hand, and on top it said – God I hated that old man – it said 'Chips with everything'. Chips with every damn thing. You breed babies and you eat chips with everything.

(*Enter* HILL.)

HILL. I said ten thirty lights out, didn't I? Ten thirty I said. I want to see you move to that hut like wind from a duck's behind –

WILFE. And O Jesus mother, that's fast mother, that's eight weeks and that's fast!

HILL. That's fast, that's fast, into the hut and move that fast. Into the hut, into the hut, in, in, into the hut. (*Looks at watch. Pause.*) Out! I'll give you . . .


Scene 3

*Parade Ground: morning.*

HILL. Out! I'll give you sixty seconds or you'll be on a charge, one, two, three, four – come on out of that hut, twenty-five, twenty-six, twenty-seven, twenty-eight. AT THE DOUBLE! Now get into a line and stop that talking, get into a line. A straight line you heaving nig-nogs, a straight line.

This is the square. We call it a square-bashing square. I want to see you bash that square. Right, now the first thing you've got to know, you've got to know how to come to attention, how to stand at ease and easy, how to make a right turn and how to step off.

Now to come to attention you move smartly, very smartly, to this position: heels together. STOP THAT! When I was born I was very fortunate, I was born with eyes in the back of my neck and don't be cheeky. Legs apart and wait till I give the command SHUN. When I give the command SHUN, you will move sharply, very sharply, to this position. Heels together and in a line, feet turned out to an angle of thirty degrees, knees braced, body erect and with the weight balanced evenly between the balls of the feet and the heels.

Shoulders down and back level and square to the front. Arms hanging straight from the shoulders.

Elbows close to the sides.

Wrists straight.

Hands closed – not clenched.

Back of the fingers close to the thighs.

Thumbs straight and to the front, close to the forefinger and just behind the seam of the trousers. Head up, chin in, eyes open, steady and looking just above their own height. Come on now, heels together, body erect and evenly balanced between the balls of the feet and the heels – you didn't know you had balls on your feet did you – well you have, use them.

Stand up straight there – keep your mouth shut and your eyes open and to the front. Right, well, you are now standing – somewhat vaguely – in the position of attention.

To stand at ease you keep the right foot still and carry the left foot to the left so that the feet are about – do it with me – so that the feet are about twelve inches apart. At the same time force the arms behind the back, keeping them straight, and place the back of the right hand in the palm of the left, thumbs crossed, fingers and hands straight and pointing towards the ground. At the same time transfer the weight of the body slightly to the left so as to be evenly balanced. Keep your arms straight and don't bend at the waist. (*Inspects them.*) Right hand inside your left, *your* left not his. Try to make your elbows meet.

When you hear me give the command SQUAD, I want you to jump to that position, smarten up, as if you were going somewhere. We'll try it – stand easy, relax, just relax, but keep your hands behind your back, don't slouch, don't move your feet and don't talk – just relax, let your head look down, RELAX! IF YOU DON'T RELAX I'LL PUT YOU ON A CHARGE!

Squad, squad – SHUN! As you were, I want you to do it together. Squad – SHUN! As you were. Squad – SHUN! STAND AT EASE!

To make a Right Turn: keeping both knees straight, turn through ninety degrees to the right swivelling on the heel of the right foot and the toe of the left raising the toe of the right and the heel of the left in doing so. Keeping the weight of the body on the right foot, on completion of this movement the right foot is flat on the ground, the left leg to the rear and the heel raised – both knees braced back and the body in the position of attention. Bring the left foot into the right, good and hard, and for the time being I want that left knee good and high, slam your foot in good and hard and keep still.

Squad, squad – SHUN.

Turning to the right – RIGHT TURN.

All right you creepy crawly nig-nogs, moon men that's what you are, moon men. I want it done together. As you were.

Squad, turning to the right – RIGHT TURN.

Now, to Step Off: When I say by the front – quick march, I don't want your pretty left foot forward anyways, like this, no, it's got to be scorching smart, like a flash of greased lightning. ONE! Like this. (*Petrified stance of a man about to step off.*) ONE! Like that, and I want that left hand up as high as you can get it and your right level with your breast pocket.

Now, on the word – MARCH – I want you only to take a step forward, *not* to march. I want you only to take a step forward, just pretend, got that? Some dim-witted piece of merchandise is sure to carry on. Now then, watch it. SQUAD – by the front – quick MARCH!

(*Sure enough two boys march off and collide with those standing still, and one in the front marches off out of sight.*)

Stop that laughing. I'll charge the next man I see smile.

(*Stands, watching the other one disappear.*)

All right, Horace, come back home. (*Airman returns, sheepishly.*) You nit, you nit, you creepy crawly nit. Don't you hear, don't you listen, can't you follow simple orders, CAN'T YOU? Shut up! Don't answer back! A young man like you, first thing in the morning, don't be rude, don't be rude. No one's being rude to you.

Stop that laughing. I'll charge the next man I see smile. (*To* SMILER.) You, I said wipe off that smile. I said wipe it off.

SMILER. I'm not smiling, Corporal, it's natural, I was born with it.

HILL. Right then, don't ever let me see that face frown or I'll haul you over the highest wall we've got. (*Approaching one*

19

*of the two marching ones.*) You. If you'd been paying attention you might 'ave done it correctly, eh? But you weren't, you were watching the little aeroplanes, weren't you? You want to fly? Do you want to reach the thundering heavens, my little lad, at an earlier age than you imagined, with Technicolor wings? KEEP YOUR EYES ON ME. (*To all.*) You better know from the start, you can have it the hard way or you can have it the easy way, I don't mind which way it is. Perhaps you like it the hard way, suits me. Just let me know. At ease everyone. Now, we'll try and make it easier for you. We'll count our way along. We'll count together, and then maybe we'll all act together. I want everything to be done together. We're going to be the happiest family in Christendom and we're going to move together, as one, as one solitary man. So, when I say 'attention' you'll slam your feet down hard and cry 'one'. Like this. And when I say 'right turn' you'll move and bang your foot down and cry 'one–pause–two'. Like this. Is that clear? Is that beyond the intellectual comprehensibilities of any of you? Good! SQUAD – wait for it – atten-SHUN!

SQUAD. ONE!

HILL. As you were, at ease. Did I say slam? Didn't I say slam? Don't worry about the noise, it's a large square, no one will mind. Squad – atten-SHUN.

SQUAD. ONE!

HILL. As you were. Let's hear that 'one'. Let's have some energy from you. I want GOD to hear you crying 'ONE, ONE, ONE – pause – TWO!' Squad – atten-SHUN!

SQUAD. ONE!

HILL. Right TURN!

SQUAD. ONE – pause – TWO!

HILL. By the left – quick – MARCH!

(*The boys march off round the stage, sound of marching and the chanting of* 'One, One, One – pause – Two! One, One, One – pause – Two!')

## Scene 4

*Sound of marching feet. Marching stops. The lecture hall. Boys enter and sit on seats. Enter* WING COMMANDER, *boys rise.*

WING COM. Sit down, please. I'm your Wing Commander. You think we are at peace. Not true. We are never at peace. The human being is in a constant state of war and we must be prepared, each against the other. History has taught us this and we must learn. The reasons why and wherefore are not our concern. We are simply the men who must be prepared. You, why do you look at me like that?

PIP. I'm paying attention, sir.

WING COM. There's insolence in those eyes, lad – I recognize insolence in a man; take that glint out of your eyes, your posh tones don't fool me. We are simply the men who must be prepared. Already the aggressors have a force far superior to ours. Our efforts must be intensified. We need a fighting force and it is for this reason you are being trained here, according to the best traditions of the R.A.F. We want you to be proud of your part, unashamed of the uniform you wear. But you must not grumble too much if you find that government facilities for you, personally, are not up to standard. We haven't the money to spare. A Meteor, fully armed, is more important than a library. The C.O. of this camp is called Group Captain Watson. His task is to check any tendency in his officers to practical jokes, to discountenance any disposition in his officers to gamble or to indulge in extravagant expenditure; to

21

endeavour, by example and timely intervention, to promote a good understanding and prevent disputes. Group Captain Watson is a busy man, you will rarely see him. You, why are you smiling?

SMILER. I'm not, sir, it's natural. I was born like it.

WING COM. Because I want this taken seriously, you know, from all of you. Any questions?

WILFE. Sir, if the aggressors are better off than us, what are they waiting for?

WING COM. What's your name?

WILFE. 247 Seaford, sir.

WING COM. Any other questions?

(*Exits. Enter* SQUADRON LEADER. *The boys rise.*)

SQN LDR. Sit down, please. I'm your squadron leader. My task is not only to ensure respect for authority, but also to foster the feelings of self-respect and personal honour which are essential to efficiency. It is also my task to bring to notice those who, from incapacity or apathy, are deficient in knowledge of their duties, or who do not afford an officer that support which he has a right to expect or who conduct themselves in a manner injurious to the efficiency or credit of the R.A.F. You are here to learn discipline. Discipline is necessary if we are to train you to the maximum state of efficiency, discipline and obedience. You will obey your instructors because they are well-trained, you will obey them because they can train you efficiently, you will obey them because it's necessary for you to be trained efficiently. That is what you are here to learn obedience and discipline. Any questions? Thank you.

(*Exits. Enter* PILOT OFFICER. *The boys rise.*)

P.O. Sit down please. I'm your pilot officer. You'll find that I'm amenable and that I do not stick rigidly to authority. All I shall require is cleanliness. It's not that I want rigid men, I want clean men. It so happens, however, that you cannot have clean men without rigid men, and cleanliness requires smartness and ceremony. Ceremony means your webbing must be blanco'd, and smartness means that your brass – all of it – must shine like silver paper, and your huts must be spick and span without a trace of dust, because dust carries germs, and germs are unclean. I want a man clean from toe nail to hair root. I want him so clean that he looks unreal. In fact I don't want real men, real men are dirty and nasty, they pick their noses – and scratch their skin, I want unreal, super-real men. Those men win wars, the others die of disease before they reach the battle-fields. Any questions? You, what are you smiling at?

SMILER. I'm not, sir, it's natural. I was born like that.

P.O. In between the lines of that grin are formed battalions of microbes. Get rid of it.

SMILER. I can't, sir.

P.O. Then never let me hear of you going sick.

(*Exits. Enter* P.T. INSTRUCTOR, FLT SGT.)

N.C.O. As you were. I'm in charge of physical training on this camp. It's my duty to see that every minute muscle in your body is awake. Awake and ringing. Do you hear that? That's poetry! I want your body awake and ringing. I want you so light on your feet that the smoke from a cigarette could blow you away, and yet so strong that you stand firm before hurricanes. I hate thin men and detest fat ones. I want you like Greek Gods. You heard of the Greeks? You ignorant troupe of anaemics, you were brought up on tinned beans and television sets, weren't you? You haven't had any exercise since you played knock-a-down-ginger, have you? Greek Gods, you hear me? Till the sweat pours out of you like Niagara Falls. Did you hear that poetry? Sweat like Niagara Falls! I don't want your stupid questions!

(*Exits.*)

PIP. You have babies, you eat chips and you take orders.

CHAS. Well, look at you then, I don't see you doing different.

    (*They march off. Sound of marching feet.*)

## Scene 5

*Sound of marching feet and the men counting. The hut. Billet inspection.* ANDREW, *the hut orderly, tidying up. Enter* P.O.

ANDREW (*saluting*). Good morning, sir.

P.O. Haven't you been told the proper way to address an officer?

ANDREW. Sorry, sir, no, sir, not yet, sir.

    (P.O. *walks around.* ANDREW *follows awkwardly.*)

P.O. There's dust under that bed.

ANDREW. Is there, sir?

P.O. I said so.

ANDREW. Yes, you did, sir.

P.O. Then why ask me again?

ANDREW. Again, sir?

P.O. Didn't you?

ANDREW. Didn't I what, sir?

P.O. Ask me to repeat what I'd already said. Are you playing me up, Airman? Are you taking the mickey out of me? I can charge you, man. I can see your game and I can charge you.

ANDREW. Yes, you can, sir.

P.O. Don't tell me what I already know.

ANDREW. Oh, I wouldn't, sir – you know what you already know. I know that, sir.

P.O. I think you're a fool, Airman. God knows why the Air Ministry sends us fools. They never select, select is the answer, select and pick those out from the others.

ANDREW. What others, sir?

P.O. Don't question me!

ANDREW. But I was only thinking of –

P.O. You aren't paid to think, Airman, don't you know that? You aren't paid to think. (*Long pause.*) No, it's no good trying that line. (*Sits.*) Why pretend? I don't really frighten you, do I? I don't really frighten you, but you obey my orders, nevertheless. It's a funny thing. We have always ruled, but I suspect we've never frightened you. I know that as soon as I turn my back you'll merely give me a V sign and make a joke of me to the others, won't you? And they'll laugh. Especially Thompson. He knows you're not frightened, that's why he's in the ranks. But I'll break him. Slumming, that's all he's doing, slumming. What's your name?

ANDREW. Andrew McClore, sir.

P.O. I don't suppose Thompson's really slumming. There *is* something about you boys, confidence, I suppose, or cockiness, something trustworthy anyway. I can remember enjoying the N.A.A.F.I. more than I do the Officers' Mess. What was your job?

ANDREW. Electrician, sir.

P.O. My father was an electrician. He used to play the piano. He really played beautifully. Tragic – my God – it was tragic.

ANDREW. Had an accident, sir?

P.O. That would be your idea of tragedy, wouldn't it? My father never had that sort of accident; he couldn't, he owned the factory he worked for. It's the other things that happen to people like him. The intangible accidents. No, his fingers remained subtle till he died, and he touched the keys with love whenever he could, but no one heard him. That was the tragedy, Andrew. No one heard him except – four uncaring children and a stupid wife who saw no sense in it. God, Andrew, how I envied that man. I could have bought so much love with that talent. People don't give

25

love away that easily, only if we have magic in our hands or in our words or in our brush then they pay attention, then they love us. You can forget your own troubles in an artist's love, Andrew; you can melt away from what you were and grow into a new man. Haven't you ever wanted to be a new man? (*Places hand on* MCCLORE's *knee.*)

ANDREW. Don't do that, please, sir.

P.O. (*change*). Don't ever rely on this conversation, don't ever trust me to be your friend. I shall not merely frighten you, there are other ways – and you will need all your pity for yourself. I warn you not to be fooled by good nature, we slum for our own convenience.

(*Enter a* FLIGHT SERGEANT.)

FLT SGT. When is – I beg your pardon, sir.

P.O. You can take over now, Flight. (*Exits.*)

FLT SGT. When is this place going to be straight?

ANDREW. Pardon, Sergeant?

FLT SGT. FLIGHT Sergeant!

ANDREW. Sorry, FLIGHT Sergeant.

FLT SGT. When is this place going to be straight, I asked?

ANDREW. I've just straightened it, Serg – er Flight – er Flight Sergeant.

FLT SGT. You what? If I come in here tomorrow and I can't eat my dinner off that floor I'll have you all outside on fatigues till midnight. Have you got that?

ANDREW. Yes, Flight Sergeant.

FLT SGT. Well, keep it. Tight! Tight! Tight, tight –

('Tight, tight, tight', *mixes to sound of marching feet, men counting.*)


Scene 6


*The billet at night. The boys are tired. Beds are being made, brasses, shoes, webbing attended to.*

26

ANDREW. And then he says 'I shall not merely frighten you, there are other ways, and you will need all your pity for yourself.' Man, I tell you it was him was frightened. A tall meek thing he is, trying to impress me.

HILL. It's not him you want to be frightened of, it's royalty. Royalty! I hate royalty more than anything else in the world. Parasites! What do they do, eh? I'm not in this outfit for them, no bloody fear, it's the people back 'ome I'm here for, like you lot. Royalty –

PIP. Good old Corporal Hill, they've made you chase red herrings haven't they?

ANDREW. And he had something to say about you too, Pip Thompson. He said you were slumming, laddie, slumming, he said 'Thompson knows you're not frightened, that's why he's in the ranks – but he's slumming.'

PIP. So he thinks you're not frightened? He's right – you're not, are you? But there *are* other ways – he's right about that too.

DODGER. You know, I've been looking at this hut, sizing it up. Make a good warehouse.

GINGER. A good what?

DODGER. Warehouse. It's my mania. My family owns a pram shop, see, and our one big problem is storage. Prams take up room, you know. Always on the lookout for storage space. Every place I look at I work out the cubic feet, and I say it will make a good warehouse or it won't. Can't help myself. One of the best warehouses I ever see was the Vatican in Rome. What you laughing at? You take a carpenter – what does he do when he enters – what does he do when he enters a room, eh? Ever thought about that? He feels how the door swings open, looks straight across to the window to see if the frame is sitting straight and then sits in the chair to see if it's made good – then he can settle down to enjoy the evening. With me it's

27

pregnant women. Every time I see pregnant women I get all maternal. You ean have your women's breasts all you want and her legs. *Me*, only one spot interests me – one big belly and we've made a sale. Can't help it – warehouses and pregnant women.

DICKEY. Hey, Cannibal my dear associate, what are you so engrossed in?

CANNIBAL. It's a book about ideal marriage, now leave me be.

DICKEY. Why you dirty-minded adolescent you – put it away.

DODGER. Here, let's have a read.

(*He and some others crowd round to read on.*)

PIP. 252 WINGATE! (*Chas automatically springs to attention.*) give me a hand with this bed, will you, please.

CHAS. Why I bloody help you I don't know, not at all I don't.

PIP. Because you like me, that's why.

CHAS. *Like* you? Like *you*? You're the lousiest rotten snob I know.

PIP. And you like snobs.

CHAS. Boy, I hate you so much it hurts. You can't even make a bed properly.

PIP. It was always made for me.

CHAS. There you go. See what I mean. Boasting of your bleedin' wealth and comfort. Well, I don't want to know about your stinking comforts, don't tell me, I don't want to hear.

PIP. Oh, yes you do. You love to hear me talk about my home. We have a beautiful home, Charles, twenty-four rooms, and they're all large and thick with carpets.

CHAS. Modern?

PIP. No, built in the time of George III.

CHAS. I don't want to know.

PIP. They started to build it in 1776 when George Washington was made Commander-in-Chief of the American Colonists and the great grandfathers of the Yanks were issuing the Declaration of Independence. A jubilant period, Charles – exciting. Did you know that while my great-great-grandfather was trading with the East India Company in the land of the strange chocolate people, bringing home the oriental spoils, the American grandfathers were still struggling to control a vast land at a time when there was no communication? But they didn't struggle long. Each time my great-grandfather came home he heard more bad news about those traitorous Americans. Returning from India in 1830, with a cargo of indigo, he heard, twenty-three years after everyone else, that the steamboat had been invented. Terrible news. Returning in 1835 with a cargo of teak they told him about the strange iron horse that ran on wheels. Terrible, terrible, news. Returning in 1840 with a cargo of correander he was so enraged that he refused to believe it possible to send messages through the air, and so he died without ever believing in the magic of the telegraph. What do you think of that, Charles boy? Still, my favourite relative was his father, a beautiful boy, the kind of boy that every aunt wanted to mother and every cousin wanted to marry. The only thing was he was incredibly stupid, much more than you, Charles, and strangely enough he was called Charles also. My family talk about him to this very day. You see, the fact was that very few people ever realized he was so stupid because he was such a handsome boy and very rarely spoke. And because of his silence everyone thought he was very wise, and this was so effective that he increased our family fortune by double. (*Nearly everyone is listening to him by now.*) You want to know how? Well, it was like this. Shortly after the shock of losing America, the English were disturbed by another event – another shock that rocked the whole of Europe and set my family and all their friends shaking. One day, the French kings and princes found themselves bankrupt – the royalty and the clergy never used to pay any taxes, you see they left that on the shoulders of the middle class and the commoners, and yet they still managed to become bankrupt. So what did they do? They called a meeting of all the representatives of all the classes to see what could be done – there hadn't been such a meeting for over a century, what a party! What a mistake! because, for the first time in a long while, the commoners not only found a means of voicing their discontent over the paying of taxes, but they suddenly looked at themselves and realized that there were more of them than they ever imagined – and they weren't fools. Now, they voiced themselves well, and so loudly that they won a victory, and not simply over the tax problem, but over a dozen and one other injustices as well. Big excitement, jubilation, victory! In fact, they found themselves so victorious and so powerful that they were able to cut off the heads of poor Louis XVI and Marie Antoinette and start what we all know as the French Revolution.

CHAS. What about Charlie, the silly one?

PIP. Patience, my handsome boy, don't hurry me. Now, my family had a lot of interest in France and its royalty, so they decided to send this beautiful boy out to see what was happening to their estates and fortunes. And do you think he did? Poor soul, he couldn't understand what the hell was happening. The royalty of all Europe was trembling because of what the French did to Louis and Marie, and he just thought he was being sent on a holiday. To this day we none of us know how he escaped with his life – but, not only did he escape with his life he also came back with somebody else's life. A French princess! And would you believe it, she was also a simpleton, a sort of prototype deb with a dimple on her left cheek. Her family had given her all their jewels, thinking that no one would touch her, since she was so helpless, and indeed no one did. No one, that is, except our Charles. He met her on his way to Paris in a Franciscan monastery and asked her to teach him French. There were her relatives being beheaded one by one and there was she, chanting out the past tense of the verb 'to be'. You can guess the rest, within four weeks he was back in England with a lovely bride and £400,000 worth of jewellery. They built a new wing to the house and had seven children. The rooms glitter with her chandeliers, Charlie boy – and – well, just look at the way your mouth is gaping – you'll get lockjaw.

HILL. Don't you tell stories, eh? Don't you just. I bet you made that one up as you went along.

PIP. That's right, Corporal, the French Revolution was a myth.

CHAS. Tell us more, Pip, tell us more stories.

PIP. They're not stories, Charlie boy, they're history.

CHAS. Well, tell us more then.

PIP. What's the use?

CHAS. I'm asking you, that's what's the use. *I'm* asking *you*.
(PIP *picks up his webbing to blanco. The others withdraw and pick up what they were doing.* CHARLIE *is left annoyed and frustrated.* HILL *takes a seat next to the fire and plays a mouth-organ. In between sounds he talks.*)

HILL. I was pleased with you lads today. You're coming on. When you did those last about turns I felt proud. You might even be better than the last lot we had. Know that? And by Christ that last lot were good. But there's one of you needs to buck up his ideas, I shan't mention names.

SMILER. I try, Corporal.

HILL. Well, you want to try harder, my son. Look at you.

SMILER. I look at myself every day, Corporal.

HILL. That stupid smile of yours, if only you didn't smile so much. Can't you have an operation or something? I'll go bleedin' mad looking at that for another five weeks.

DODGER. Oh, my gawd, listen to this! Listen what it says here.

C

'Between 200 and 300 million spermatozoa are released at one time of which only one succeeds in fertilizing the female ovum.' Jesus! All them prams!

GINGER. Give us a good tune, Corp, go on.

HILL. You're my treasure, aren't you, eh, Ginger lad? Don't know what I'd do without you. What shall I play for you, you name it, I'll play it.

GINGER. Play us the 'Rose of Tralee'.

HILL. You want the 'Rose of Tralee', my beauty? You shall have it then.

(CORPORAL HILL *plays, the boys rest, work, write letters, and listen.*)

GINGER. When's the Christmas Eve party?

DODGER. Tomorrow a week, isn't it?

HILL. Uh-huh.

(*Continue sound of mouth-organ – change to –* )


### Scene 7

*The N.A.A.F.I. Christmas Eve Party. The rock'n'roll group play vigorously. The boys jiving, drinking and singing. Officers are present.*

WING COM. Look at them. Conscripts! They bring nothing and they take nothing. Look at them. Their wild dancing and their silly words – I could order them at this moment to stand up and be shot and they'd do it.

SQN LDR. You're drinking too much, Sid.

WING COM. Civilians! How I hate civilians. They don't know – what do they know? How to make money, how to chase girls and kill old women. No order, no purpose. Conscripts! They bring their muddled lives and they poison us, Jack; they poison me with their indifference, and all we do is guard their fat bellies. I'd sacrifice a million of them for the grace of a Javelin Fighter, you know that?

SQN LDR. Don't let them see you scowl. Smile, man, smile. It's a Christmas Eve party. We're guests here.

SMILER (*to* WILFE). Go and offer the Wing Commander a drink, then, go on.

WILFE. Leave off, will you, man? All evening you have been pestering me. What do I want to go giving officers drinks for?

SMILER. Go up to him and say 'with the compliments of our hut, sir', go on.

WILFE. I'll pour a bottle on you soon if you don't leave off.

SMILER. Your fly button's undone.

WILFE. Where? Smiler, I'll bash you – you tantalize me any more this evening and I'll bash that grin right down to your arse, so help me, I will.

SMILER. Listen to him. Wilfe the warrior. Do you talk like this at home? Does your mummy let you?

WILFE. Now why do you talk to me like that? Why do you go on and on and on? Do I start on you like that? Take this away, will you boys, take him away and drown him.

SMILER. Go after one of them N.A.A.F.I. girls, go on, Wilfe. Go and find out if they're willing.

CANNIBAL. N.A.A.F.I. girls! Camp bloody whores, that's all they are.

DICKEY. Well, he's woken up. Cannibal has spoken, come on, me ole cocker, say more.

CANNIBAL. Who's for more drink?

DICKEY. Good old Cannibal! He uttered a syllable of many dimensions. The circumlocircle of his mouth has moved. Direct yourself to the bar, old son, and purchase for us some brown liquid. We shall make merry with your generosity.

CANNIBAL. I don't know where he gets the words from. He lies in his bed next to me and he talks and he talks and he sounds like an adding-machine.

DICKEY. You're under-educated, my old son – you're devoid of knowledgeable grey matter. You should've gone to a technical school like me; we sat in study there and ate up books for our diluted pleasure. We developed voluble minds in that technical college and we came away equipped with data. Data! That's the ticket – the sum total of everything. Direct your attention to the bar, I say, and deliver us of that inebriating liquid, my hearty.

CANNIBAL. Ask him what he means. Go on, someone? I don't know. He lies on his bed next to me and he talks and he mumbles and talks and he mumbles. One night he woke up and he shouted: 'Kiss me, Mother, kiss your dying son.'

DICKEY. You lie in your teeth, O dumb one. Buy the drinks.

CANNIBAL. And another night he crept up to me and he was crying. 'Let me in your bed,' he moaned, 'let me get near you, you're big and warm.'

DICKEY. You're lying, Cannibal. Don't let me hear more of your lies.

CANNIBAL. Shall I tell them how you pray at nights?

(DICKEY *throws his beer over* CANNIBAL *and they fight.*)

WING COM. Separate those men! Hold them! Stop that, you two, you hear me, an order, stop that! (*They are separated.*) Undisciplined hooligans! I won't have fighting in my camp. Is this the only way you can behave with drink in you? Is it? Show your upbringing in your own home where it grew but not here, you hear me? Not here! This is Christmas Eve. A party, a celebration for the birth of our Lord, a time of joy and good-will. Show me good-will then. I will not, will not, will not tolerate your slum methods here. This is a clean force, a clean blue force. Go to your huts, stay there, stay there for the rest of the evening and don't wander beyond ten feet of your door. Disobey that order and I shall let out the hell of my temper so hard that you'll do jankers the rest of your National Service.

(DICKEY *and* CANNIBAL *leave. On the way*, DICKEY *trips over, and* CANNIBAL *helps him to his feet.*)

WING COM. They don't even fight seriously – a few loud words, and then they kiss each other's wounds. God give us automation soon.

SQN LDR. You suffer too much, Sid.

WING COM. Nonsense! And forget your theories about my unhappy childhood. Mine is a healthy and natural hatred.

SQN LDR. I haven't time to hate – it takes me all my time to organize them.

WING COM. Look at them. What are they? The good old working class of England. Am I supposed to bless them all the time for being the salt of the earth?

SQN LDR. They provide your food, they make your clothes, dig coal, mend roads for you.

WING COM. Given half the chance you think they would? For me? Look at them, touching the heights of ecstasy.

PIP. They're talking about us – the officers.

CHAS. What are they saying?

PIP. They're saying we're despicable, mean and useless. That fight disturbed the Wing Commander – he looks like my father.

ANDREW. Did you join us just on account of your father?

PIP. Is that what it looks like?

ANDREW. Love on the rebound, man, not much cop you know. Don't do us any favours.

PIP. Don't start on me, Andy, there's a good man. I don't have to drop my aitches in order to prove friendship, do I?

ANDREW. No. No, you don't. Only I've known a lot of people like you, Pip. They come drinking in the pub and talk to us as though we were the salt of the earth, and then, one day, for no reason any of us can see, they go off, drop us as though that was another game they was tired of. I'd give a pension to know why we attract you.

WING COM. What do you know about that one, Jack, the one with the smart-alec eyes and the posh tones?

SQN LDR. Thompson? Remember, General Thompson, Tobruk, a banker now?

WING COM. So that's the son. Thompson! Come here, Airman.

PIP. Sir?

WING COM. Enjoying yourself?

PIP. Thank you, sir.

WING COM. Gay crowd, eh?

PIP. I imagined you would dislike conscripts, sir.

WING COM. I haven't met you before, Thompson; your father impressed me but you don't.

PIP. Is that all, sir?

WING COM. I can have you, boy. I can really have you – remember that.

CHAS. What'd he want, Pip, what'd he say?

PIP. He wouldn't dare. Yes, he would. He's going to test you all. The old fool is really going to experiment. I wonder what method he'll choose.

WILFE. What d'you mean, experiment, what experiment?

PIP. How he hates you; he's going to make an announcement; whatever happens, do as I tell you – don't question me, just do as I tell you.

ANDREW. If you have a war with that man, Pip, don't use me as <u>fodder</u>, I'm warning you.

PIP. Help, Andy, I'm helping, or do you want to be made fools of?

WING COM. Silence everybody, your attention please, gentlemen – Thank you. As you all know we hoped, when we organized this gay gathering for you, that we'd have a spot in the evening when everyone would get up and do a

36

turn himself. A dirty recitation, or a pop song. I'm sure that there's a wealth of native talent among you, and now is the chance for you to display it in all its glory, while the rest of us sit back and watch and listen. My officers are always complaining of the dull crowds we get in this camp, but I've always said no, it's not true, they're not dull, just a little inhibited – you – er know what inhibited means, of course? So now's the time to prove them wrong and me right. You won't let me down, will you, lads? Who's to be first? Eh? Who'll start?

PIP. Very subtle, eh, Andy?

WILFE. Will someone tell me what's going on here? What's so sinister about a talent show?

WING COM. The first, now.

PIP. Burns, Andrew –

ANDREW. Burns?

PIP. Your bloody saint, the poet –

ANDREW. I know he's a poet but –

PIP. Recite him, man, go on, get up there and recite.

ANDREW. Recite what? I –

PIP. In your best Scottish accent now.

ANDREW. Hell, man (*once there*) I – er – Burns. A poem. (*Recites it all, at first hesitantly, amid jeers, then with growing confidence, amid silence.*)

> This ae nighte, this ae nighte,
> *Every nighte and alle,*
> Fire and fleet and candle-lighte,
> *And Christe receive thy saule.*

> When thou from hence away art past,
> *Every nighte and alle,*
> To Whinny-muir thou com'st at last;
> *And Christe receive thy saule.*

37

If ever thou gavest hosen and shoon,
*Every nighte and alle,*
Sit thee down and put them on;
*And Christe receive they saule.*

If hosen and shoon thou ne'er gav'st nane
*Every nighte and alle,*
The whinnes sall prick thee to the bare bane;
*And Christe receive thy saule.*

From Whinny-muir when thou art past,
*Every nighte and alle,*
To Purgatory fire thou com'st at last;
*And Christe receive thy saule.*

If ever thou gavest meat or drink,
*Every nighte and alle,*
The fire sall never make thee shrink;
*And Christe receive thy saule.*

If meat or drink you ne'er gav'st nane,
*Every nighte and alle,*
The fire will burn thee to the bare bane
*And Christe receive thy saule.*

This ae nighte, this ae nighte,
*Every nighte and alle,*
Fire and fleet and candle-lighte,
*And Christe receive thy saule.*

(*Ovation.*)

WING COM. Come now, something more cheerful than that.
How about a song – something from Elvis Presley.
(*Band and Boys begin pop song.*)

PIP. Not that, not now.

WING COM. Lovely, yes, that's it, let's see you enjoying yourselves.

38

PIP. Don't join in boys – believe me and don't join in.

WILFE. What *is* this – what's going on here?

WING COM. Look at them – that's them in their element.

PIP. Can't you see what's happening, what he's thinking?

WING COM. The beer is high, they're having a good time.

PIP. Look at that smug smile.

WING COM. Aren't they living it up, just, eh? Aren't they in their glory?

PIP. He could lead you into a swamp and you'd go.

WING COM. Bravo! Bravo! That's the spirit! Make merry – it's a festive occasion and I want to see you laughing. I want my men laughing.

    (*Loud pop song. Pip moves to guitarist and whispers in his ear. Boy protests, finally agrees to sing* 'The Cutty Wren', *an old peasant revolt song. Boys join in gradually, menacing the officers.*)

ALL.

### THE CUTTY WREN

'Where are you going?' said Milder to Malder,

'We may not tell you,' said Festle to Fose,

'We're off to the woods,' said John the Red Nose,

'We're off to the woods,' said **John the** Red Nose.

'What will you do there?' said Milder to Malder.
'We may not tell you,' said Festle to Fose.
'We'll shoot the cutty wren,' said John the Red Nose,
'We'll shoot the cutty wren,' said John the Red Nose.

'How will you shoot him?' said Milder to Malder.
'We may not tell you,' said Festle to Fose.
'We've guns and we've cannons,' said John the Red Nose,
'We've guns and we've cannons,' said John the Red Nose.

'How will you cut her up?' said Milder to Malder.
'We may not tell you,' said Festle to Fose.
'Big hatchets and cleavers,' said John the Red Nose,
'Big hatchets and cleavers,' said John the Red Nose.

'How will you cook her?' said Milder to Malder.
'We may not tell you,' said Festle to Fose.
'Bloody great brass cauldrons,' said John the Red Nose,
'Bloody great brass cauldrons,' said John the Red Nose.

'Who'll get the spare ribs?' said Milder to Malder.
'We may not tell you,' said Festle to Fose.
'Give them all to the poor,' said John the Red Nose,
'Give them all to the poor,' said John the Red Nose.

WING COM. Quite the little leader, aren't you, Thompson? Come over here, I want a word with you in private. Stand to attention, do your button up, raise your chin – at ease. Why are you fighting me, Thompson? We come from the same side, don't we? I don't understand your reasons, boy – and what's more you're insolent. I have every intention of writing to your father.

PIP. Please do.

WING COM. Oh, come now. Listen, lad, if you've got a fight on with your father that's all right by me, we all fight our fathers, and when we fight them we also fight what they stand for. Am I right? Of course I'm right. I understand you, boy, and you mustn't think I'm unsympathetic. But it's not often we get your mettle among conscripts – we need you. Let your time here be a truce, eh? Answer me, boy, my guns are lowered and I'm waiting for an answer.

PIP. Lowered, sir?

WING COM. You know very well what I mean.
(WING COMMANDER *and* OFFICERS *leave*.)

HILL. Well, a right mess you made of that interview. If there's any repercussions in our Flight, if we get victimized cos of you, boy, I'll see you –

PIP. Don't worry, Corp, there won't be any repercussions.

CHAS. Well, what in hell's name happened – what was it all about?

SMILER. This party's lost its flavour – let's go back to the hut, eh? I've got a pack of cards – let's go back and play cards.

CHAS (*of* PIP). Talk to him is like talking to a brick wall. PIP!

Scene 8

*The N.A.A.F.I.*

PIP. You've got enemies, Charles boy. Learn to know them.
(*The others have gone.*)

CHAS. Enemies? I know about enemies. People you like is enemies.

PIP. What do *you* mean when you say that, Charles?

CHAS. Oh, nothing as clever as you could mean, I'm sure.

PIP. Come on, dear boy, we're not fighting all the time, are we? You mustn't take too much notice of the way I talk.

CHAS. You talk sometimes, Pip, and I don't think you know that you hurt people.

PIP. Do I? I don't mean to

CHAS. And sometimes there's something about your voice, the way you talk – that – well, it makes me want to tell you things.

PIP. You were telling me about enemies you like.

CHAS. You're embarrassed.

41

PIP. You were telling me –

CHAS. Now why should I embarrass you?

PIP. – enemies you like.

CHAS. No, about people you liked who were enemies. There's a difference. I'm surprised you didn't see the difference.

PIP. Go on.

CHAS. Go on what?

PIP. What do you mean?

CHAS. Mean?

PIP. What you just said.

CHAS. Well, I said it. That's what it means.

PIP. Oh, I see.

CHAS. I do embarrass you, don't I?

PIP. A bit. Are you an only child, Charles?

CHAS. I got six brothers. You?

PIP. Four brothers.

CHAS. What I meant was people say things meaning to help but it works out all wrong.

PIP. You could have meant a number of things, I suppose.

CHAS. Words do mean a number of things.

PIP. Yes, Charles.

CHAS. Well, they do.

PIP. Mm. I'm not sure why we started this.

CHAS. Well, you said we got enemies, and I was saying –

PIP. Oh, yes.

CHAS. There, now you've lost interest. Just as we were getting into conversation you go all bored.

PIP. Don't nag at me, Charles.

CHAS. Charlie.

PIP. Oh, I can't call you Charlie – it's a stupid name.

CHAS. Now why did you have to say that? Making a rudeness about my name. Why couldn't you leave it alone. I want to be called Charlie. Why couldn't you just call me Charlie? No, you had to criticize.

42

PIP. All right, Charlie then! Charlie! If you don't mind being called Charlie you won't ever mind anything much.

CHAS. You're such a prig – I don't know how you can be such a barefaced prig and not mind.

PIP. I'm not a prig, Charles, that's so suburban – a snob perhaps but nothing as common as prig, please. Tell you what, I'm a liar.

CHAS. A liar?

PIP. Yes – I haven't got four brothers – I'm an only son.

CHAS. So am I.

PIP. You? Yes – I might've guessed. Poor old Charlie. Terrible, isn't it? Do you always try to hide it?

CHAS. Yes.

PIP. Not possible though, is it?

CHAS. No. Funny that – how we both lied. What you gonna do when they let us out of camp?

PIP. When is it?

CHAS. Next Friday.

PIP. Oh, go into the town, the pictures perhaps.

CHAS. Can I come?

PIP. Yes, I suppose so.

CHAS. Suppose so! You'd grudge your grandmother a coffin.

PIP. But I've just said you could come.

CHAS. Yes, dead keen you sounded.

PIP. Well, what do you want?

CHAS. Don't you know?

PIP. Oh, go to hell!

CHAS. I'm sorry, I take it back, don't shout. I'll come – thanks. (*Pause.*) If I was more educated you think it'd be easier, wouldn't it, between us?

PIP. What do you mean 'us'? –

CHAS. Let me finish –

PIP. For God's sake don't start wedding me to you –

CHAS. Just let me –

43

PIP. And don't whine –

CHAS. You won't let me –

PIP. You are what you are – don't whine.

CHAS. Let me bloody finish what I was going to say, will you! You don't listen. You don't bloody listen.

PIP. I'm sorry –

CHAS. Yes, I know.

PIP. I'm listening.

CHAS. Oh, go to hell – you –

PIP. I'm sorry, I take it back, don't shout, I'm listening.

CHAS. I didn't say *I* thought it'd be easier if I was more educated – I said *you'd* think it'd be easier, I thought *you'd* think it. And I was just going to say I disagreed – then you jumped.

PIP. Yes, well, I thought – yes, well, you're right Charles, quite right. It's no good wanting to go to university –

CHAS. Facts, that's all it is.

PIP. Like me and work – manual labour. The number of intellectuals and artists who are fascinated by manual labour. Not me though, Charles. I haven't the slightest desire to use my brawn, prove myself a man, dirty my nails.

CHAS. And facts don't mean much to me either.

PIP. It's dull, repetitive, degrading.

CHAS. Intelligence counts, not facts. Stick your education, your university. Who cares why Rome was built.

PIP. Van Gogh with the miners; Hemingway, hunting.

CHAS. Even if I knew all about that it wouldn't make it any easier.

PIP. God, how I despise this yearning to be one of the toilers.

CHAS. I knew someone who used to wear a bowler cos he thought it made him look educated.

PIP. The dignity of labour!

CHAS. But it wouldn't make it any easier –

44

PIP. The beauty of movement!
CHAS. Not between us –
    (*They smile.*)


Scene 9

*The Hut.*

SMILER. What shall it be – poker, pontoon?
WILFE. I'm for bed.
SMILER. 'I'm for bed', little boy is tired.
WILFE. You can go on man – nothing seems to affect you.
CANNIBAL. What happened? They kick you out too?
SMILER. We got sick – you game for poker?
DICKEY. The squalor overcame you, eh? Ah, well, welcome
    back to the delinquents.
    (*Enter* HILL.)
HILL. Well, I've got a right bunch, haven't I, a real good
    crowd, that's a fact.
GINGER. Come off it, Corp – you know we're O.K. on the
    square.
DODGER. That's all that counts, isn't it, Corp?
HILL. My boys – even them, my own little boys let me down.
SMILER. It's poker, Corp, you playing?
HILL. I shan't say anything now because you're away home in
    two days – but when you come back it's rifle drill and
    bayonet practice – and that's tough, and if you slack – I'm
    warning you – no more easy life, it'll be back to normal
    for you all.
DODGER. Play us a tune, Corp.
HILL. You don't deserve no tunes – a kick up the arse you
    deserve, the lot, where it hurts, waken you up.
    (CHARLES, SMILER, PIP *and* DICKEY *sit down to play. The*

*others lie in their beds, and* HILL *plays the mouth-organ.*)

GINGER. There's a bloody great moon outside. Dodge, you seen it? With a whopping great halo.

DODGER. Nippy, too. Who wants some chocolate? My uncle has a sweet shop. (*Produces dozens of bars.*)

DODGER. Ging, what trade you going to apply for?

GINGER. Driver – I'm going to get something out of this mob – it's going to cost them something keeping me from civvy street. Driving! I've always wanted to drive – since I don't know how long. A 6 BP engine, behind the wheel controlling it – nyaaaaaaaaaaaarr. I dream about it. I dream I'm always in a car and I'm driving it, but I got no licence. I always know I've never driven a car, but somehow it comes easy to me and I've never got a ruddy licence. I'm always being chased by cops – and I keep dreaming it, the same dream. I got no licence, but I'm driving a car and the police are after me. What'll I dream about when I can drive a car, I wonder.

DODGER. You won't. Stands to reason you won't need to; when you got the real thing you don't pretend. How about some tea? Ginger, my cock, make some tea on the stove and we'll eat up these biscuits also.

CANNIBAL. Dreams is real you know, they may be pretending in your sleep, but they're real. I dreamt my girl was a prostitute once and when I see her next day she looked like one and I give her up.

DODGER. What's wrong with prostitutes? We need them, let's keep them I say. Nationalize them. Stuck in clubs like poor bleedin' ferrets.

WILFE. Don't it make you sick, eh? Don't it make you sick just – these eight weeks, these two years, the factory – all of it? Don't it make you just bleedin' sick? I SAID SICK, MOTHER, SICK! Poor dear, she can't hear a word.

(*Pause. Mouth-organ. Warm hut.*)

46

CANNIBAL. I'm going to get in that Radar-Plotting lark. All them buttons, them screens and knobs. You have to learn about the stars and space for that.

DICKEY. That's astronomy, my fine fellow. The code of the heavens. Radar! Radar is the mystic digits of sound-waves; you have to have an enlightened degree of knowledge for that. Cannibal, my son, you're not arrogant enough, not standard enough for that. But I could – oh yes, I could rise to the heights of radar. I've put in for that.

SMILER. I think I'll go into Ops. Bring the planes in. Operations calling D17, are you receiving me, are you receiving me – over! D17 calling flight-control, I'm receiving you – left jet gone, I said gone, think I'll have to make a forced landing, stand by for emergency. Nyaaaaaaah passssssssssss, brrrrrrrrrrrrrrrrr – we'll all learn a trade and then 'oppit – nyaaaaaaaaaaaaaaa . . .

(Pause.)

ANDREW. I like us. All of us, here now. I like us all being together here. In a way you know I don't mind it, anything. Old Corp and his mouth-organ – all of us, just as we are, I like us.

(Pause. Mouth-organ. Warm hut.)

GINGER. We've run out of coke you know – water won't ever boil.

PIP. Then we'll pinch some.

DICKEY. What?

PIP. That's all right with you isn't it, Corp? You don't mind a little raiding expedition?

HILL. You think you'll get in the coke yard? You won't, you know, mate; there's a wire netting and a patrol on that.

PIP. We'll work out a plan.

CHAS. Oh, knock it off, Pip, we're all in bed soon.

PIP. Think we can't outwit them?

DODGER. You won't outwit them, mate, they've got it all tied up neat, not them me old *lobus*.

PIP. If you can't outwit them for a lump of coke, then they deserve to have you in here for a couple of years.

HILL. I know what you are, Thompson – you're an agent provocative.

WILFE. I'm game, how do we do it?

GINGER. We could snip the wire and crawl through.

PIP. No. We want to raid and leave no sign.

ANDREW. What do we put it in?

DICKEY. Buckets.

DODGER. Too noisy.

PIP. Buckets with sacking at the bottom. How high is the netting?

HILL. About six feet. You'll need a ladder.

WILFE. Take it from the fire hut near by.

CANNIBAL. What if there's a fire?

WILFE. Let it burn.

PIP. No, no risks. Efficient, precise, but humane. They happen to be the only qualities for absolute power. That's what we want – absolute success but without a price. Coke in ten minutes, with no one caught and no one but us the wiser. Trust me?

## Scene 10

*A large square of wire netting. A* GUARD *walks round it. Boys are in the shadows.*

PIP. Now watch him – he walks round slowly – we can make three moves for each round except the last one and that requires speed. I want the first three stages started and finished between the time he disappears round the first corner and before he turns the third. If he changes his course or hurries his step or does anything that means one of us is caught, then we all, all of us make an appearance. He can't cop the lot. Right? (*All exit.*)

(GINGER *dashes to wire, and places chair – dashes to other side of stage. PIP runs to chair, jumps up and over. DODGER runs to take chair away and joins GINGER. The GUARD appears and carries on round. DODGER runs back, places chair. WILFE runs to chair with another, jumps on it and drops chair into PIP's hands, runs off. DODGER runs on, and withdraws chair. The GUARD appears, and continues. DODGER runs on with chair again. ANDREW runs with buckets to chair, jumps up and passes them to PIP. GINGER runs to take chair away. GUARD appears, and continues. In like process, two buckets are returned 'full' of coke. In the last stage, PIP jumps back over netting, leaving chair. GINGER and DODGER appear with two stools. DICKEY dashes on to top of two stools, leans over wire and reaches down for chair, which he throws to ANDREW. DODGER and GINGER run off with two stools. GUARD appears, and continues. This scene can be, and has to be, silent, precise, breathtaking and finally very funny.*

## Scene 11

*The hut again. Mouth-organ. DODGER pouring out tea, drinking, eating. Silence.*

DICKEY. Yes. Yes – very satisfactory. Very pleasing. I wouldn't've thought we could do it.

CHAS. No more you wouldn't have done it without Pip.

DICKEY. Do I detect in young Charles the ineffable signs of hero worship?

49

CHAS. You'll detect black and blue marks, that's what you'll detect.

DICKEY. I think we've got a love affair in our midst.

CHAS. Just because I respect a man for his nerve? You gone daft?

DICKEY. No, I think my mental balance is equilibralized, it's you I fear for my Charlie boy. First you start off bating young Thompson here and now you can't take your eyes off him.

PIP. Don't act the goat, Dickey.

DICKEY. I'm correct in my observations though aren't I, Lord Thompson?

PIP. No observation you make is correct, Dickey, you just remember other people's.

DICKEY. But you have a marvellous mind don't you?

CHAS. He has.

DICKEY. Now there's a question. Would we have pinched the coke without Pip's mind?

HILL. You always need leaders.

PIP. Always!

HILL. Well, don't you always need leaders?

PIP. Always, always!

HILL. Yes, always, always!

PIP. Always, always, always! Your great-great-grandfather said there'll always be horses, your great-grandfather said there'll always be slaves, your grandfather said there'll always be poverty and your father said there'll always be wars. Each time you say 'always' the world takes two steps backwards and stops bothering. And so it should, my God, so it should –

WILFE. Easy, Airman, easy.

GINGER. Hey, Dodge – come and look outside now. Have you ever seen a halo as big as that? – look at it.

DODGER. Means frost.

ANDREW.    This ae nighte, this ae nighte,
     *Every nighte and alle,*
Fire and fleet and candle-lighte,
     *And Christe receive thy saule.*

SLOW CURTAIN

# ACT TWO

## Scene 1

*The hut, dark early morning. Enter night* GUARD.

GUARD. Hands off your cocks and pull up your socks, it's wake to the sun and a glorious day. (*Pulls off blankets of one near by.*) Rise, rise, rise and shine – Christmas is over. CHRISTMAS IS OVER. (*Exits.*)

    (*There have been moans and movements. Return to silence. Enter* HILL. *Pause.*)

HILL. CHRISTMAS IS OVER, he said.

    (*Moans and movements.*)

It's over, done, finished. You're 'ome. You're 'ome again and it's rifles today. Rifles and a stricter routine. You've been slacking. I've warned you and told you and today is judgment day, especially for you, Smiler – today is especially judgment day for you. You too, Airmen Wilfe, Seaford and Archie Cannibal, you shan't be passed. I intend making you the smartest squad in the glorious history of flying – and I will. But you – AC/2 Thompson – you're too good for me, too smart. The wing commander and all the officers in charge of this camp have got their guns on you and they're aiming to throw the book at you – the whole, heavy scorching book, so you beware and guard your mouth. I've heard, I know – so guard your mouth. CHRISTMAS IS OVER. (*Exits.*)

WILFE. Christmas is over and don't we know it. Rouse yourself, Smiler, or you'll get us all in the cart.

SMILER. Leave off.

WILFE. Rouse yourself, I say – I aren't suffering cos of you. Get up or I'll turn you under your bed.

    (*No reply.* WILFE *does so.* SMILER *rises from under the*

52

*rubble and angrily fights with* WILFE *till separated by others.*)

ANDREW. Cut it out or I'll lay you both.

DICKEY. Its the basic animal rising to undiluted heights in them. A nasty morning, my boys, a nasty morning, nasty tempers and a nasty undiluted life.

CANNIBAL. And you can shut your undiluted mouth for a start, too. I'm not stomaching you the rest of the time.

DICKEY. What side of the bed did you rise from?

CANNIBAL. I'm fit for you, so don't worry.

(*Enter* HILL *with rifles.*)

HILL. Come and get them. Don't grab them, don't drop them and don't lose them. We start with them first thing after breakfast and I intend to train you so hard that you'll not be happy unless they're in bed with you.

(*Exit. Immediately, half the boys start playing cowboys and indians, dropping behind beds and crawling on the floor, firing them at each other.* 'BANG. BANG.' *Enter* HILL.)

HILL. The next man to pull that trigger, his feet won't touch the ground.

(SMILER *clicks one unintentionally.*)

You – I've wanted to pounce on you, Smiler.

SMILER. It slipped, Corp – an accident.

HILL. You say accident, I say luck. I'm charging you, Smiler, just a little charge, a few days' jankers to start with – that's all.

PIP. Why don't you charge us all, Corporal?

HILL. YOU SHUT UP. You, I've warned. All of you, I've warned. The joke's over, the laughing's done. Now get ready. (*Exits.*)

DODGER. We used to have a master who'd crack a joke, and then look at his watch to see we didn't laugh too long.

HILL. All right, get fell in, the lot of you.

53

## Scene 2

*The parade ground. The men in threes.*

HILL. The first thing is – not to be afraid of it. It won't hurt you and if you handle it correctly you can't hurt it. (*Only one boy laughs.*) I know you think they're nice, boys. With one of them in your hand you feel different, don't you, you feel a man, a conquering bloody hero? You want to run home and show your girl, don't you? Well, they're not toys – you can kill a man wi' one o' them. Kill 'im! Your napkins are still wet – you don't really understand that word 'kill', do you? Well, you can be killed. There! Does that bring it home to you? A bullet can whip through your flesh and knock breath out of *you*. Imagine yourself dying, knowing you're dying, you can feel the hole in your body, you can feel yourself going dizzy, you can feel the hot blood and you can't breathe. You want to breathe but you can't, the body you've relied on all these years doesn't do what you want it to do, and you can't under-stand it. You're surprised, you're helpless, like those dreams where you're falling – only dying isn't a dream because you know, you know, you know that you're looking at everything for the last time and you can't do a bloody thing about it, that's dying. And that's a rifle. So don't let me catch anybody aiming it at anybody – loaded or not. Now, you hold it here, just below the barrel, pushing it out slightly to the right and forward, with the butt, tucked well in at the side of your feet – so – well in firm, straight, at ease – and at the command to 'shun' I want that rifle brought smartly in at the precisely same moment. So. Atten-tion! Together, and your hand holding firmly on to that rifle. I don't want that rifle dropped – drop that rifle and I want to see you follow it to the ground. Right. Squad – atten-tion!

54

SQUAD. One!

(SMILER *drops gun.*)

HILL. Leave it! Smiler, you nasty squirming imbecile! Can't you hear me? Can't you hear anything? Don't anything go through your thick skull? Look at you. Slob! Your buttons, your blanco, your shoes – look at them. They're dull. You're dull! You're like putty. What keeps you together, man? You're like an old Jew – you know what happens to Jews? They go to gas chambers. Now pick it up. Squad – atten-tion!

SQUAD. One!

HILL. Now to slope and shoulder arms, you make three move-
ments. Watch me, follow me and you won't make a mess of it. I'll do it slowly and I'll exaggerate the movements. Shoulder ARMS! One pause, two pause, three. Slope ARMS! One pause, two pause, three. Again. (*Repeats.*) Now – you do it. Squad! Shoulder ARMS!

SQUAD. One pause, two pause, three.

HILL. Slope ARMS!

SQUAD. One pause, two pause, three.

(*Repeats order.*)

HILL. You're no good, Smiler, you're no good. Shoulder ARMS! Smiler, one pace forward march. The rest, about turn. By the left, quick march.

(*The squad march off, all except* SMILER. *The wall of the guard-room drops into place as scene changes to –* )


Scene 3


*The guard-room.* SMILER *at the slope. Enter* HILL *and two other corporals.*


1ST CORP. This him?

HILL. That's him.

2ND CORP. What's your name, lad?

SMILER. Smiler.

2ND CORP. I said your name, lad.

SMILER. 279 AC/2 Washington, Corporal.

1ST CORP. Washington, is it? You mustn't lie then, ha-ha! If
you mustn't lie, then tell us, is your mother pretty? Is she?
Answer me, lad. Do you know it's dumb insolence not
to answer an N.C.O.? We'll make that six days' jankers,
I think. Answer me, lad.

SMILER. Yes. She was.

1ST CORP. Have you ever seen her undressed? Eh? Have you,
lad? Have you seen her naked?

2ND CORP. Wipe that smile off your face, lad.

SMILER. I'm not smiling, Corporal, it's natural. I was born
like it.

1ST CORP. Arguing with an N.C.O. We'll make that nine days'
jankers.

HILL. All right Smiler, order arms, slope arms, order arms,
slope arms, slope arms, slope arms.

(*The two corporals walk round him.*)

1ST CORP. You're a slob, Smiler.

2ND CORP. A nasty piece of work.

1ST CORP. You're no good, lad.

2ND CORP. No good at all. You're an insult.

1ST CORP. Your mother wasted her labour.

2ND CORP. Your father made a mistake.

1ST CORP. You're a mistake, Smiler.

2ND CORP. A stupid mistake.

1ST CORP. The Queen doesn't like mistakes in her Air Force.

2ND CORP. She wants good men, Smiler, men she can trust.

1ST CORP. Stand still, boy. Don't move. Silent, boy. Still and
silent, boy.

HILL. That'll do for a taster, Smiler. That'll do for the first lesson. Tomorrow we'll have some more. We'll break you, Smiler, we'll break you, because that's our job. Remember that, just remember now – remember – About TURN! By the left – quick march, eft – ite, eft – ite. Remember, Smiler, remember.

(*Exit.*)


## Scene 4

WING COMMANDER'S *office. With him at a table are* SQUADRON LEADER *and* PILOT OFFICER.

WING COM. Just remember who we're dealing with – remember that. I don't want a legal foot put wrong – I just want him broken in.

P.O. Not broken in, sir, but loved – he's only lost temporarily, for a short, natural time, that's all.

WING COM. Bloody little fool – sowing seeds of discontent to semi-educated louts; what do they understand of what he tells them?

SQN LDR. Gently, Sid, anger'll only make it easier for him to be stubborn.

P.O. Leave it to me, sir. I think I know how to do it, I think I know the boy very well.

WING COM. I know the boy, by Christ I know him, I've known them all and I've broken them all.

(HILL *marches* PIP *into the room.*)

PIP. You called me to see you, sir.

WING COM. Take your hat off, blast you, Thompson, take it off, lad, in front of an officer.

SQN LDR. Please sit down, won't you, Thompson, sit down and and be at ease for a little while; we'd simply like a chat with you.

WING COM. Your square bashing is coming to an end. We're concerned about you. We have to find you something to do. It has to be decided now.

SQN LDR. I think, Wing Commander, if you'll excuse me, it would be more correct to say that personnel must decide that in London, but we can recommend from here, isn't that the case? We are on the spot, so we can recommend.

P.O. We see, Thompson, that you've put down administration orderly as your first and only choice. A very strange choice.

WING COM. A damn fool choice, boy, your brains, your carriage and background, damn perversity!

SQN LDR. You know what administration orderly implies, don't you, son?

WING COM. Anything and everything – waste, absolute waste.

SQN LDR. Anything from dish-washing to salvage, from spud-bashing to coal-heaving.

(*Pause.*)

P.O. Listen Pip, excuse me, sir?

WING COM. Yes, yes, carry on.

P.O. Let's drop the pretence. We're the same age and class, let's drop this formal nonsense. The Air Force is no place to carry on a family war, Pip. This is not a public school, it's a place where old boys grow into young men, believe me. Don't force me to start listing all your virtues and attributes. We're not flatterers, but don't let's be falsely modest either – that's understood between us, I'm sure. God, when I think of what I did to try and get out of coming into this outfit – two years wasted I thought. But waste is what you yourself do with time – come on man, if people like us aren't officers, then imagine the bastards they'll get. This is a silly game, Pip – why look, you're even sulking. Admin orderly! Can you see yourself washing dishes?

PIP. It might be a pretence to avoid responsibility.

P.O. You, Pip? Come now! It may be that you want to prove something to yourself. I don't know, why don't you tell us?

PIP. Your tactics are obvious, please don't insult my intelligence. I do not feel obliged to explain my reasons to you.

WING COM. You'll do what you're told.

P.O. It's not a question of obligation, no one's forcing –

PIP. I have no wish to –

P.O. But there's no one forcing you –

PIP. I said I have no wish to –

P.O. But-no-one-is-forcing-you –

PIP. I have no wish to explain anything to you I say.
    (*Pause.*)

WING COM. Corporal Hill!
    (*Enter* HILL.)

HILL. Sir?

WING COM. The men in your squad are slobs. Their standard is low and I'm not satisfied. No man passes out of my camp unless he's perfect – you know that. Pull them together, Corporal Hill, fatigues, Corporal Hill. They're a wretched bunch, wretched, not good enough.

HILL. Yes, sir. (*Exits from room.*)
    All right, fall in, the lot of you.
    (*Boys enter.*)
    You're slobs, all of you. Your standard is low and I'm not satisfied. No man passes out of my hut unless he's perfect, I've told you that before. You're a wretched bunch – a miserable, wretched bunch, and since you're not good enough, it's fatigues for you all. Squad will double mark time.
    (*They do so for one minute. Exit at the double. The Inquisition resumes.*)

WING COM. Carry on, P.O.

P.O. Right, Thompson, I have some questions to ask you. I

don't want clever answers. You wish to be an administration orderly?

PIP. That is correct, sir.

P.O. Doesn't it occur to you that that very act, considering who you are, is a little – revealing? It's a rather ostentatious choice, isn't it?

PIP. It could be viewed like that.

P.O. You enjoy mixing with men from another class. Why is this? Do you find them stimulating, a new experience, a novelty, do you enjoy your slumming?

PIP. It's not *I* who slum, sir.

P.O. I suppose you feel guilty in some way for your comfortable and easy upbringing; you feel you must do a sort of penance for it.

PIP. A rather outdated cause to be a martyr for, don't you think, sir?

P.O. Possibly, Thompson, possibly. You enjoy their company, though, don't you?

PIP. I enjoy most people's company.

P.O. Not ours, though.

PIP. Certain standards are necessary, sir.

P.O. A very offensive reply, Thompson – it's almost a hysterical reply – a little too desperately spoken, I would say. But look, we haven't stiffened, we aren't offended, no one is going to charge you or strike you. In fact we haven't really taken any notice. We listen to you, we let other people listen to you but we show no offence. Rather – we applaud you, flatter you for your courage and idealism but – it goes right through us. ⟨We listen but we do not hear,⟩ we befriend but do not touch you, we applaud but we do not act. To tolerate is to ignore, Thompson. You will not really become an administration orderly, will you?

PIP. What I have written, stays.

P.O. You will not be a foolish, stiff, Empire-thumping officer –

no one believes in those any more. You will be more subtle
and you will learn how to deal with all the Pip Thompsons
who follow you. I even think you would like that.

PIP. What I have written stays. You may recommend as you
please.

P.O. Yes, we shall put you up for officer training.
   (OFFICERS *exit. Scene changes to –* )

### Scene 5

*The Square. A dummy is hanging. It is bayonet practice for the squad.*

HILL. Even officers must go through this. Everyone, but
   everyone must know how to stick a man with a bayonet.
   The occasion may not arise to use the scorching thing but
   no man passes through this outfit till he's had practice.
   It's a horrible thing, this. A nasty weapon and a nasty way
   to kill a man. But it is you or him. A nasty choice, but you
   must choose. We had a bloke called Hamlet with us once
   and he had awful trouble in deciding. He got stuck! I don't
   want that to be your fate. So! Again, hold the butt and
   drop the muzzle – so. Lean forward, crouch and let me see
   the horriblest leer your face can make. Then, when I call
   'attack' I want to see you rush towards that old straw
   dummy, pause, lunge and twist your knife with all the
   hate you can. And one last thing – the scream. I want to
   hear you shout your lungs out, cos it helps. A hoard of
   screaming men put terror in the enemy and courage in
   themselves. It helps. Get fell in, two ranks. Front rank will
   assume the on-guard position – ON GUARD! Run,
   scream, lunge.
      (HILL *demonstrates it himself. One by one, the men rush*
      *forward at the dummy, until it comes to* PIP. *He stands still.*)
   I said attack. Thompson, you, that's you. Are you gone

61

daft? I've given you an order – run, scream, you. Are you refusing to obey? AC Thompson I have ordered you to use your bayonet. You scorching, trouble-making, long-haired, posh-tongued, lump of aristocracy – I'll high jump you, court martial you. I'll see you rot in every dungeon in the force. Oh, thank your lucky stars this ain't the war, my lad; I'd take the greatest pleasure in shooting you. You still refuse? Right – you men, form up a line behind this man; I'll need you all for witnesses. AC/2 Thompson, I am about to issue you with a legitimate order according to Her Majesty's rules and regulations, Section 10 paragraph 5, and I must warn you that failing to carry out this order will result in you being charged under Section 10 paragraph 16 of the same book. Now, when I say attack, I want to see you lower your gun in the attack position and race forward to lunge that dummy which now faces you. Is that order understood?

PIP. Yes, Corporal.

HILL. Good. I am now about to give the command. Wait for it and think carefully – this is only practice and no one can be hurt. Within ten seconds it will all be over, that's advice. Attack.

(*Silence. No movement.*)

Squad – slope ARMS! AC/2 Thompson – I'm charging you with failure to obey a legitimate order issued by an N.C.O. in command under Her Majesty's Air Force, and may God help you, lad.

(*All march off except* THOMPSON.)

## Scene 6

*Enter* ANDREW.

ANDREW. Idiot.

62

PIP. You?

ANDREW. Who the hell is going to be impressed?

PIP. You, Andrew?

ANDREW. Yes, Andrew! I'm asking you – who the hell do you think is going to be impressed? Not me. The boys? Not them either. I've been watching you, Pip – I'm not impressed and neither are they.

PIP. You don't really think I'm interested in the public spectacle, Andy, you can't? No, no I can see you don't. Go off now. Leave me with it – I've got problems.

ANDREW. No one's asking you to make gestures on our behalf.

PIP. Go off now.

ANDREW. Don't go making heroic gestures and then expect gratitude.

PIP. Don't lean on me, Andy – I've got problems.

ANDREW. I don't think I can bear your martyrdom – that's what it is; I don't think I can bear your look of suffering.

PIP. I'm not suffering.

ANDREW. I don't know why but your always-acting-right drives me round the bend.

PIP. I'm not a martyr.

ANDREW. It's your confident cockiness – I can't stand your confident cockiness. How do you know you're right? How can you act all the time as though you know all right from wrong, for God's sake.

PIP. Don't be a bastard Jock.

ANDREW. I'm trying to help you, idiot. The boys will hate any heroic gesture you make.

PIP. Andy, you're a good, well-meaning, intelligent, person. I will die of good, well-meaning and intelligent people who have never made a decision in their life. Now go off and leave me and stop crippling me with your own guilt. If you're ineffectual in this world that's your look-out – just stay calm and no one will know, but stop tampering with my decisions. Let *them* do the sabotaging, they don't need help from you as well. Now get the hell out – they wouldn't want you to see the way they work.

(*Exit* ANDREW.)

## Scene 7

*Enter* P.O.

P.O. It goes right through us, Thompson. Nothing you can do will change that. We listen but we do not hear, we befriend but do not touch you, we applaud but do not act – to tolerate is to ignore. What did you expect, praise from the boys? Devotion from your mates? Your mates are <u>morons</u>, Thompson, morons. At the slightest hint from us they will disown you. Or perhaps you wanted a court martial? Too expensive, boy. Jankers? That's for the yobs. You, we shall make an officer, as we promised. I have studied politics as well, you know, and let me just remind you of a tactic the best of revolutionaries have employed. That is to penetrate the enemy and spread rebellion there. You can't fight us from the outside. Relent boy, at least we understand long sentences.

PIP. You won't impress me with cynicism, you know.

P.O. Not cynicism – just honesty. I might say we are being unusually honest – most of the time it is unnecessary to admit all this, and you of all people should have known it.

PIP. I WILL NOT BE AN OFFICER.

P.O. Ah. A touch of anger, what do you reveal now, Thompson? We know, you and I, don't we? Comradeship? Not that, not because of the affinity of one human being to another, not that. Guilt? Shame because of your fellow beings' suffering? You don't feel that either. Not guilt. An inferiority complex, a feeling of modesty? My God. Not that either. There's nothing humble about you, is there? Thompson, you wanted to do more than simply share the joy of imparting knowledge to your friends; no, not modesty. Not that. What then? What if not those things, my lad? You and I? Shall I say it? Shall I? Power. Power, isn't it? Among your own people there were too many who were powerful, the competition was too great, but here, among lesser men – here among the yobs, among the good-natured yobs, you could be king. KING. Supreme and all powerful, eh? Well? Not true? Deny it – deny it, then. We know – you and I – we know, Thompson.

PIP. Oh, God –

P.O. God? God? Why do you call upon God? Are you his son? Better still, then. You are found out even more, illusions of grandeur, Thompson. We know that also, that's what we know, that's what we have, the picture you have of yourself, and now that we know that, you're really finished, destroyed. You're destroyed, Thompson. No man survives whose motive is discovered, no man. Messiah to the masses! Corporal Hill! (*Exits.*)

HILL (*off stage*). Sir?


Scene 8


*Enter Hill.*


HILL. I have instructions to repeat the order, Thompson. The powers have decided to give you another chance. I don't know why, but they know what they're doing, I suppose. When I give the order 'attack' I want you to lean forward, run, thrust and twist that blade in the dummy. Have you understood?

PIP. Yes, Corporal.

65

HILL. Run, thrust and twist that blade – good. ATTACK.
(*Pip pauses for a long while, then with a terrifying scream he rushes at the dummy, sticking it three times, with three screams.*)

### Scene 9

*The hut.* CHARLES *and* PIP.

CHAS. What they say, Pip? What they want you for, what did they say? Hell, look at your face, did they beat you? Did they make you use the bayonet? They did, didn't they? I can tell it from your face. You're crying – are you crying? Want a cigarette? Here, have a cigarette. The others have all gone to the N.A.A.F.I., it's New Year's Eve, gone for a big booze-up. Bloody fools – all they do is drink. I think I'll give it up, me. Well, what did they say, man – talk to me? You know why I didn't go to the N.A.A.F.I. – I – I was waiting for you. It seemed fishy them calling you in the evening, so I waited to see. Pip? I'm telling you I waited for you. I wanted to tell you something, I want to ask you a favour; I've been meaning all these last days to ask you this favour. You see – you know me, don't you, you know the sort of bloke . . . I'm – I'm, I'm not dumb, I'm not a fool, I'm not a real fool, not a bloody moron and I thought, well, I thought maybe you could, could teach me – something, anything. Eh? Well, not anything but something proper, real.

PIP. Ask someone else – books, read books.

CHAS. Not books! I can't read books, but I can listen to you. Maybe we'll get posted to the same place, and then every evening, or every other evening, or once a week, even, you could talk to me a bit, for half an hour say. Remember how you talked that night about your grandfathers, about all those inventions and things. Well, I liked that, I listened to that, I could listen all night to that. Only I want to know about something else, I want to know about – I don't even know how to put it, about – you know, you know the word, about businesses and raw materials and people working and selling things – you know, there's a word for it –

PIP. Economics.

CHAS. Enocomics – that's it.

PIP. Economics not enocomics.

CHAS. EE-mon-omics.

PIP. No, Ee –

CHAS. Ee

PIP. Con

CHAS. Con

PIP. Om

CHAS. Om

PIP. Ics.

CHAS. Ics.

PIP. Economics.

CHAS. Economics. There, about that, could you? I'd listen, you could draw diagrams and graphs; I wasn't bad at maths.

PIP. Someone else, Charles, not me, someone else.

CHAS. There you go. You're a hypocrite – a hypocrite you are. You take people to the edge. Don't you know what I'm asking you, don't you know what I'm really asking you?

PIP. Ask someone else.

CHAS. But I want to be with you – I want to. Ah, you give me a pain in the neck, you do, you're a coward. You lead and then you run away. I could grow with you, don't you understand that? We could do things together. You've got to be with someone, there's got to be someone you can trust, everyone finds someone and I found you – I've never asked anyone before, Jesus, never –

PIP. Ask someone else.

CHAS. Someone else. Someone else. It's always someone else, you half-bake you, you lousy word-user you. Your bleedin' stuffed grandfathers kept us stupid all this time, and now you come along with your pretty words and tell us to fend for ourselves. You clever useless leftover you. Oh, you're cocky, aren't you – Ask someone else. The truth is – you're scared, aren't you? You call us mate, but you're a scared old schoolboy. The pilot officer was right, you're slumming. You're a bleedin' slummer –

PIP. And he also said 'we will listen to you but we will not hear you, we will befriend you but not touch you, we will tolerate and ignore you.'

CHAS. Well, what did that mean?

PIP. We'll do anything they want just because they know how to smile at us.

CHAS. You mean *I'll* do what they want, not you boy. You're one of them – you're just playing games with 'em, and us mugs is in the middle – I've cottoned on now. (*Long pause.*) I'll do what *you* want, Pip.

PIP. Swop masters? You're a fool, Charles, the kind of fool my parents fed on, you're a fool, a fool –

(*Fade in the sound of marching feet, and the Corporals repeating the insults they heaped upon Smiler and change to –* )

## Scene 10

*A roadway.* SMILER *has run away from camp. He is desperate, haggard and tired. Mix:* 'You're a fool, Charles' *to* 'You're a slob, Smiler' 'A nasty piece of work' 'You're no good, lad', *etc., rising to crescendo –*

SMILER. LEAVE ME ALONE! Damn your mouths and hell

on your stripes – leave me alone. Mad they are, they're
mad they are, they're raving lunatics they are. CUT IT!
STUFF IT! Shoot your load on someone else, take it out
on someone else, why do you want to pick on me, you
lunatics, you bloody apes, you're nothing more than
bloody apes, so damn your mouths and hell on your
stripes! Ahhhhh – they'd kill me if they had the chance.
They think they own you, think that anyone who's
dressed in blue is theirs to muck about, degrade. YOU
BLOODY APES, YOU WON'T DEGRADE ME! Oh
my legs – I'm going home. I'll get a lift and scarper home.
I'll go to France, I'll get away. I'LL GET AWAY FROM
YOU, YOU APES! They think they own you – Oh my
back. I don't give tuppence what you say, you don't mean
anything to me, your bloody orders nor your stripes nor
your jankers nor your wars. Stick your jankers on the
wall, stuff yourselves, go away and stuff yourselves, stuff
your rotten stupid selves – Ohh – Ohhh. Look at the sky,
look at the moon, Jesus look at that moon and the frost
in the air. I'll wait. I'll get a lift in a second or two, it's
quiet now, their noise is gone. I'll stand and wait and look
at that moon. What are you made of, tell me? I don't know
what you're made of, you go on and on. What grouses
you? What makes you scream? You're blood and wind
like all of us, what grouses you? You poor duff bastards,
where are your mothers? Where were you born – I don't
know what grouses you, your voices sound like dying
hens – I don't know. That bloody lovely moon is cold, I
can't stay here. I'll freeze to death. That's a laugh, now
that'd fool them. Listen! A bike, a motor-bike, a roaring
bloody motor-bike. (*Starts thumbing.*) London, London,
London, London, LONDON! (*The roar comes and dies.*)
You stupid ghet, I want a lift, can't you see I want a lift,
an airman wants a lift back home. Home, you bastard,

69

take me Ho'ooooome. (*Long pause.*) Now they'll catch me, now they'll come, not much point in going on – Smiler boy, they'll surely come, they're bound to miss you back at camp – eyes like hawks they've got – God! Who cares. 'Stop your silly smiling, Airman' – 'It's not a smile, Corp, it's natural, honest, Corp. I'm born that way. Honest Corp, it's not a smile . . .'

(*Enters hut.*)

## Scene 11

*The hut.* CHARLES *and* PIP *as we left them.* SMILER *is now with them.*

SMILER. The bastards won't believe it's natural. Look at me, me!

(*A very broken* SMILER *stands there.* SMILER *turns to* PIP *for help.* PIP *approaches him and takes him gently in his arms. They sway a moment.*)

SMILER. Wash my feet for me.

(SMILER *collapses.* PIP *lays him on the ground. He is about to remove his shoes –*)

CHAS. Leave him. I'll do it.

(CHARLES *doesn't know what to do to begin with. Surveys* SMILER. *Then – picks him up and lays him on his bed, looks at him; thinks; takes off his shoes and socks.*)

CHAS. His feet are bleeding.

(*Takes a towel and pours water from pot on it; washes* SMILER'*s feet; a long unconscious moan from* SMILER; *clock strikes midnight; sound of boys singing* 'Aulde Land Syne'. CORPORAL HILL'*s voice, loud.*)

HILL (*off stage*). You pass out with the band tomorrow – rifles, buttons, belts, shining, and I want you as one man, you hear me? You'll have the band and it'll be marvellous; only you Smiler, you won't be in it, you'll stay behind a little longer, my lad – HAPPY NEW YEAR.

(*Silence. One by one the rest of the men come in, returning from N.A.A.F.I. They make no sound, but their movements are wild and drunk. No sound at all – like a TV with sound turned off, till they see* SMILER.)

DODGER. Look at his feet. The rotten bastards, look at his feet.

ANDREW. What'd he do?

CHAS. Tried to hop it.

ANDREW. Couldn't make it?

CHAS. Walked for miles and then came back.

CANNIBAL. They had it in for him, you've got no chance when they got it in for you.

GINGER. He's staying behind, you know? I reckon they'll make him do another two weeks of this.

DICKEY. Give me the chance, just give me one chance and I'd have them. Five minutes in civvy street and I'd have them chasing their own tails.

WILFE. Ah, you wouldn't, man – you talk like this now but you wouldn't, and you know why? Cos you'd be just as helpless there, you'd be just as much wind and nothing there, man. 'Just gimme the boss,' you'd say, 'just gimme him for one hour in uniform and I'd teach him what a man is.' That's all you'd say, civvy street, the forces – it's the same, don't give me that.

GINGER. What about Smiler's stuff?

CANNIBAL. I'll do it.

CHAS. No, you won't, I'm doing it.

CANNIBAL. All right, all right, then. Blimey, what's gotten into you? Jumping at me like that – I don't much want to do my own buggers, let alone his. Takes all the guts out of you, don't it. Look at him, lying there like a bloody corpse. His feet are cold.

71

DODGER. He's like a baby. Sweet as a sleeping baby. Have you ever watched a baby sleep? It always looks as though it's waiting for something to happen, a grown-up seems to be hiding away but a nipper seems to trust you, anyone. He's done it, ain'tee, eh? He's really had it –

CHAS. For Christ's sake, give over – you talk like he was dead or something, Come on, help cover him.

(*As many as possible manoeuvre* SMILER *so that his jacket and trousers come off, with the least disturbance. This action is done lovingly and with a sort of ritual.* DODGER *takes a comb to* SMILER'*s hair and* CHARLES *gently wipes a towel over his face. Then they tuck him in bed and stand looking at him. Unknown to them the* P.O. *has been watching them.*)

P.O. Beautiful. Tender and beautiful. But I'm sorry, gentlemen, this man is needed in the guard-room.

(*Enter* HILL.)

HILL. Squad – shun!

(*The men slowly come to attention, except* CHARLES, *who, after a pause, moves to his bed and sits on it. One by one the other boys, except* PIP, *also sit on their beds in defiance.*)

P.O. Corporal – take that smiling airman to the guard-room.

CHAS. YOU'LL LEAVE HIM BE!

P.O. And take that man, too.

GINGER. You won't, Corporal Hill, will you?

P.O. And that man, take the lot of them, I'll see them all in the guard-room.

PIP. You won't touch any of them, Corporal Hill, you won't touch a single one of them.

P.O. Do you hear me, Corporal, this whole hut is under arrest.

PIP. I suggest, sir, that you don't touch one of them. (PIP *and the* P.O. *smile at each other, knowingly, and* PIP *now begins to change his uniform, from an airman's to an officer's.*) We

72

won't let him, will we Charles – because you're right.
Smiler has been badly treated and you are right to protect
him. It's a good virtue that, loyalty. You are to be com-
mended, Charles, all of you; it was a brave thing to do,
protect a friend. We lack this virtue all too often, don't
you agree, sir? These are good men, sometimes we are a
little hasty in judging them – don't you agree, sir, a little
too hasty? These are the salt of the earth, the men who make
the country, really. Don't worry, Charles, nor you,
Ginger, nor you, Andrew – none of you, don't worry,
you shan't be harmed – it was a good act. We like you for
it, we're proud of you, happy with you – you do agree,
don't you, sir? These are men we need and these are the
men we must keep. We are not hard men, Charles – don't
think ill of us, the stories you read, the tales you hear. We
are good, honest, hard-working like yourselves and understanding; above all we are understanding, aren't we, sir?
There, that's a good fit, I think. (P.O. *hands a list over to*
PIP. PIP *reads out the list.*)

PIP. 239 AC/2 Cannibal – (CANNIBAL *rises to attention.*)
administration orderly, posted to Hull. (*Stands at ease. Same
procedure for others.*)
252 AC/2 Wingate – administration orderly, posted to
Oxford.
247 AC/2 Seaford – administration orderly, Cyprus.
284 AC/2 McClure – typing pool, Malta.
272 AC/2 Richardson – administration orderly, Aden.
277 AC/2 Cohen – administration orderly, Halton.
266 AC/2 Smith – administration orderly, Lincoln.
279 AC/2 Washington – put back three weeks to flight
212 – decision of employ will be made at a later date.
Squad – Squad, SHUN.
   (*Sudden loud sound of brass band playing the R.A.F. March
   Past.*)

## Scene 12

*Music of March Past. The Parade Ground. Passout Parade. The men march into position. A flagpole is moved in.*

HILL. Squad atten-tion! Shoulder arms! Right turn! By the left mark time! Lift your heads, raise them, raise them high, raise them bravely, my boys. Eft-ite, eft-ite, eft-ite, eft. Slope that rifle, stiffen that arm – I want to see them all pointing one way, together – unity, unity. Slam those feet, slam, slam, you're men of the Queen, her own darlings. SLAM, SLAM! SLAM! Let her be proud. Lovely, that's lovely, that's poetry. No one'll be shot today, my boys. Forget the sweat, forget the cold, together in time. I want you to look beautiful, I want you to move as one man, as one ship, as one solid gliding ship. Proud! Proud! Parade, by centre, quick march, saluting to the front.

(*Men salute to audience, return back to face* WING COMMANDER. *Music stops.* WING COMMANDER *on a rostrum. Officers around him.*)

WING COM. (a long, broad embracing smile). I am satisfied. Good. Good men. One of the best bunch I've had through my gates. Smart, alert, keen. Two years of service in Her Majesty's Air Force lie ahead of you, I am confident of the service you will give, you have turned out well, as we expected, nothing else would have done, just as we expected. God speed you.

(GINGER *comes to attention. Lays rifle on ground. Steps forward to flagpole and takes ropes in his hands.*)

HILL. Parade about turn.

(*Men now face audience again.*)

SQN LDR. Parade, for colour <u>hoisting</u>. PRESENT ARMS!

(*Ginger very very slowly hoists the R.A.F. colours. Let it be a tall pole. 'The Queen' is played, and there is a –* )

SLOW CURTAIN.

74

Dec. 17, 1969